Grateful Walks

Key West Inspirations

In gratitude to my spiritual advisor Tawny,
My joyous companion Bella,
My heart's home Key West,
Nature's abundant inspirations
&
to those who choose to
see the world with kind eyes,
keep forgiving, open hearts
and share their light
as we all walk each other home.

Grateful Walk Instructions:

Decide to go

Set the intuition to leave your worries at the doorstep

Walk and look for what makes your heart smile

Feel gratitude for what you have found

Repeat

Each day I go for a grateful walk with my dog Bella.
Before I leave, I choose to set aside all my worries.
I leave them at my doorstep
offering to address what worries remain when I return.
When my worries try and follow me,
I put my hand on my heart and begin filling with gratitude.
I've noticed that worry and gratitude do not like to hang out together,
so the more I fill with gratitude
the less space there is for worry in my heart.
This benefit alone has been life-changing for me.
I've also learned the heart and gratitude have a beautiful relationship.
Whenever you send gr
atitude out,
you are sending out goodness
while at the same time
filling your own heart.
Gratitude has also led me deeper in my heart
where I learned how to see through the eyes of my heart
nature's relationship with me.
It is from this viewpoint,
that I discovered new perspectives
on how to find purpose in pain,
discover beauty in chaos,
and embrace the gifts found in change.
My narrow viewpoint widened to witness the boundless love
and endless resilience of the heart.   May this journey of deep appreciation
inspire you on your daily gratitude walks and
may your heart always overflow with gratitude.

Soulful Navigations

On this rainy morning in Key West,
I sat with the beauty of storms and how many storms that I've been
through. I cannot count the times I've drowned in my emotions and
thought the storms would never end.
But they did.
The storms ended.
I reminded myself again....
all the storms I have been through have passed.
This storm will pass as well.
Until then, I choose to let me soul be the captain.
My mind and heart keep attempting to take the helm, but in this journey
I've learned it is my soul that is the wise, weathered sailor.
She offers me buoyancy when my heart drowns in emotions.
She guides me by the stars when my mind gets too dark.
She uses the storms to throw overboard what I no longer need
in this vessel for my journey ahead.
She navigates me to deeper channels of faith and then
rests me on the shores of the next part of my life's adventure.
As we weather the current storm, may you be reminded that you have
bright stars within
to navigate you through this dark unknown territory.
May your heart stay buoyant.
May you have ease in letting go and your shores ahead
become the favorite part of your adventure.

Spiral Journey

As I came upon this shell

born in the depths of the sea,

it awakened a timeless truth of the path of life.

It often feels like I've walked this path before.

Although with the wisdom learned from the past,

I am going deeper.

I smile when I remember

the center of the spiral.

While the mind sees it as a tight enclosed place,

the soul knows its freedom is vast.

Rise and Float

Allow yourself to be embraced by life
like the humble trust of floating in the sea.
Those peaceful moments when it is just you and the sea.
You let go.
You float.
Gently being held from the bottom.
Moving yet stable.

Beauty in Change

There is beauty in change and
the sunset shows us that every night.

Synchronized Good

As I watch these fish jump together
to evade a common danger,
I honor the wisdom of their community
to collectively
work together for the common good.
-They honor each other's unique space while maintaining
their own forward direction.
-They go with the flow adapting to the sea's changing
conditions in seemingly synchronized precision.

From their wisdom,
-May we work together for the common good.
-May we honor each other's unique space while maintaining
our own forward direction.
-May we be so in tune with nature that we effortlessly
synchronize into the common flow.

Beads and Tutus

After deciding that it is difficult to be a joyful sniveler,
I see these beads and
paused to delight
at the adventures they have been on
in some Key West celebration.
I reflect on the power I've seen celebration to help
me and others to come out of our protective shells,
drop the heaviness of the roles we have been living
and feel lightness of heart again.
May you celebrate life
like you are in Key West today:
- Freely where a tutu everywhere you go
- Give beads to everyone that makes you smile
- Grab your friends and savor the sunset together
- Dance with abandon

Light in the Storm

Sometimes, taking time by the sea can
reconnect you to your inner strength.
There is power in connecting again
to what reignites your roaring passion.
Seek the light in the storm.
Let your passion roar again.

By Focus

When I find myself crashing into painful memories
and being swallowed into a dark hole,
I reach into the darkness
with the light of far I have come.
On particularly difficult days,
I start coming out of the darkness by focus.
I focus on the sensations at the moment.
The sound of a powerful breeze
that is so refreshing on my skin.
Cooling me, calming me
and offering to blow away my worries.
Sitting with what is in the present
allows my mind
to focus
on what is versus what was,
and my spirit to bathe in gratitude.

Letting Go

You deserve some time today to sit and let go.
Let go of worries of the future,
let go of the hurt of the past
and sit
in the radiance of the moment.

Little Things

"Sometimes the smallest things
take up the most room in your heart."
- Winnie the Pooh
I spent this morning's gratitude walk
focused on the little things...
-Watching Bella enjoying the flowers
-The tiny white flowers in bougainvillea
-Listening to the music of the sea as the waves rolled in
-Thanking the breeze
-The renewed faith offered as a tiny feather fell before me
All of these little things
gave me the gift
of focusing
on beauty
instead of worry
and gave my heart a big dose of gratitude.
May your day overflow
with the beauty of little things.

Divine Destruction

Constantly begging for attention,
fears of the past will begin screaming in my mind
inviting my senses to become hypervigilant
for unknown dangers in the present.
When my soul has had enough,
her winds howl and seas rage
to clear out
that which does not serve the highest good anymore.
Wisdom has taught me
to no longer resist the chaos of her clearing.
I've learned to leave the familiarity of looking out and
watch the divine destruction from the eyes of my soul.
When I resist and look out,
I grieve the ripping away of all
that I thought I needed to survive.
Looking in, I humbly smile
at how she crashes against the walls I've built
between my heart and life
to set me free.

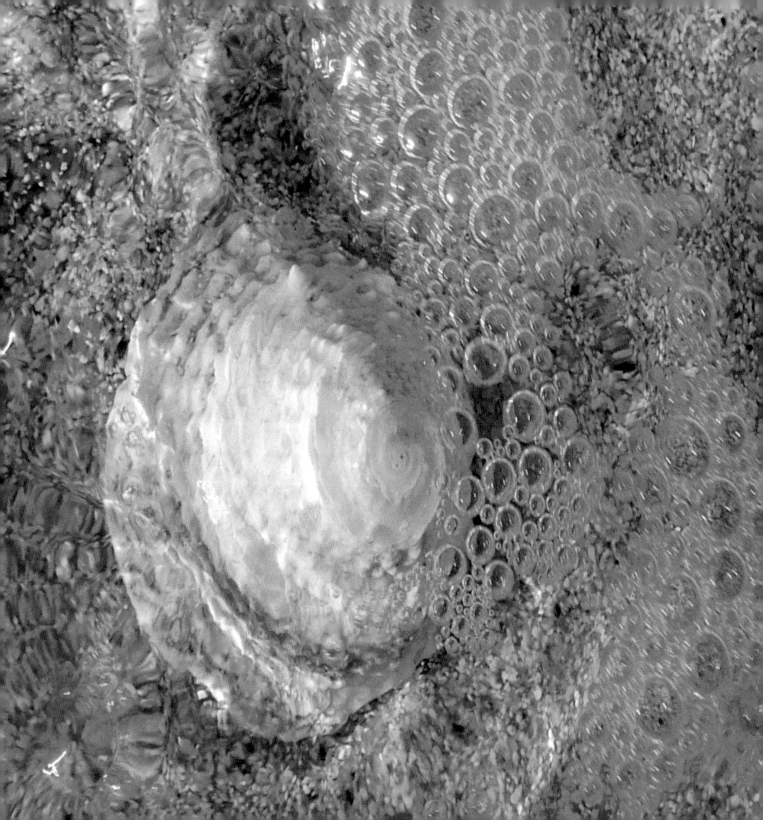

Collecting Sea Shells

The feeling of not being good enough
is an invitation
to discover
the truth
within.
Like a seashell
ready to come ashore,
my truth awaits.

Benefits of Confusion

On this wobbly pier,
I sat and found gratitude
for the most confusing people and circumstances in my life.

Because of confusion,
I began to question
what is good, right and true for my journey.
I discovered that while we are all walking each other home,
we are on different paths to get there.
I choose to trust my inner compass
to where my path is leading me.
I'm so glad I did
because it led me to where my heart knew was home.

Laugh with me

The earth laughs in flowers - Ralph Waldo Emerson

Whether you giggle with the flowers
or grin with the sea,
take some time today to
let your whole body smile.

Do it Anyway

People are often unreasonable, illogical and self centered;
Forgive them anyway.
If you are kind, people may accuse you of selfish, ulterior motives;
Be kind anyway.
If you are successful, you will win some false friends and some
true enemies;
Succeed anyway.
If you are honest, people may cheat you;
Be honest anyway.
What you spend years building, someone could destroy overnight;
Build anyway.
If you find serenity and happiness, people may be jealous;
Be happy anyway.
The good you do today, people will often forget tomorrow;
Do good anyway.
Give the world the best you have, and it may never be enough;
Give the world the best you've got anyway.
You see, in the final analysis, it is between you and your God;
It was never between you and them anyway.
-Mother Theresa

Grinning

I discovered this cheerful gecko
sunbathing
along my walk with my dog Bella.
As I thought about the beauty of this little lizard,
she smiled at me.
I stopped to appreciate her colors
and Bella attempted to taste her beauty.
She was just high enough up
that Bella could not reach her
and she looked down and grinned at Bella.
She knew danger was present
but did not choose fear as a response.
She was a role model
to trust my instincts
and stay grounded even when danger may be near.
I've been practicing this wisdom
and have found a deep appreciation
for grinning at danger

Weaving Possibilities

I get inspired by the spiny orb weaver spider's web.
I've watched her rebuild it around the yard and am
reminded how many times
I've rebuilt my life.
Remembering the difficulties I've made it through
in the past, I feel a sense of hope
in rebuilding again.
I smile at the possibilities
and remember nature releases what no longer serves
to let new life emerge.
Life may now weave in possibilities
I have never imagined.

Broken Pieces

Sometimes I've found that life breaks me and throws me into an
ocean of emotions.
I'm tossed about in
currents of loneliness,
riptides of anger
and sometimes sink in sadness.
Eventually, I wear myself out
and I discover
the joy of riding in the waves.
I learn the wisdom
that is my choice to go with the flow
or crash in resistance.
There is no judgment either way
as each way has its own lesson.
One day I find myself gently upon the shore.
I'm gleefully discovered by an appreciative soul.
She wonders how far my travels have been
and what mysteries I've uncovered in the sea.
She whispers to me how beautiful I am.
I thank the sea for making me more
humbled… softened… wiser.

Fresh eyes and purple skies

During my gratitude walk,
I asked myself to let go of the issues of the day
and the the issues of the past
so that I could begin tomorrow
with fresh eyes,
a full heart
and a clear mind.
Thank goodness it took me a while to let go
as when I finally said "yes"
to a clear new day,
I bathed in purple skies.

I will meet you there

I may walk the battered pier.
You may swim the ocean.
She may paddle her kayak.
He may sail his vessel.

Either way, we will meet again
in the wide horizon.

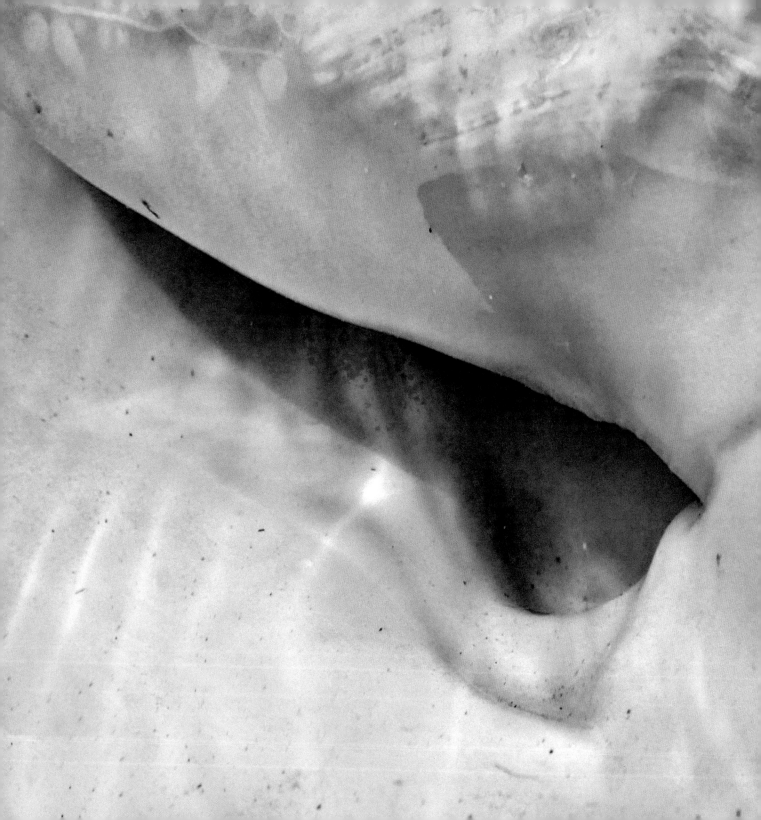

The Conch Republic

If you find a conch shell washed up on the beach,
make sure the owner has taken up a new residence.
You are holding a carefully built home constructed in the sea.
Beautifully decorated, this home is tiny yet strong.
When the owner moves out,
her home turns into a treasure for others to discover.
If you listen to her,
she will sing you songs of the sea.
You will often hear her playing music
with others to celebrate the sunset.
It is said, that her sacred songs
also welcome in new beginnings.
I've wondered if that is why Key West locals are called conchs.
In following the wisdom of conchs,
locals have beautifully decorated homes that are tiny yet strong.
You can hear us singing the songs of the sea
and celebrating the gift of the sunset every night.
We invite you to leave behind what you have outgrown
and welcome your new beginnings.
And, when you stay long enough -
you are gifted to go beyond the outer shell
and discover the gifts that are within.

Reflections

"Gratitude is the sign of noble souls."

~Aesop

Spend some time today with your heart.

Focus on what makes her grateful.

Allow her to overflow with gratitude.

Your overflowing gratitude will naturally

connect with others in appreciation

that is beyond words.

Seeing past the thorns of criticism,

the ravages of the heart

and the multitude of painful wounds of harsh battles,

gratitude holds in appreciation

who we really are.

Others will sense your gratitude

offering them a soft, kind remembrance

of who they are.

It is such a sacred gift you have to offer.

Thank you noble one!

Your wings are ready

Today I sit with gratitude for the
wisdom I learn from nature.
She holds tremendous power
but only chooses to cause destruction to
lovingly assist in growth.
A seed is destroyed to become a flower.
A butterfly must completely leave behind her life as a
caterpillar to spread her wings and fly.
Seeing nature's wisdom
gave me the gift to release
my resistance to being my natural self.
I now fondly remember the caterpillar I once was,
the struggle it took to get out of my cocoon and
bravely set out to test my wings.

Key West Goals

Choose joy
Focus on beauty
Celebrate the sunset
Bask in colors
Overflow in gratitude
Repeat

Tweet Heart

When I chose to stay open to love in all forms,
beautiful experiences happen....
like birds gathering together to share
the form of a heart with me.
I am looking forward to hearing
about the love
that happens just for you.
Today, let us choose to set the intention
to stay open
and aware
to all the unexpected and different ways
we are loved today.

My soul compass

Blindly following the path laid out by others
made my aching heart cry out to be heard.
As I listened to my heart's wisdom,
she led me off the land out into unknown waters.
As I began to move in the direction of my true North,
other hearts cried out for me to stay in ports of betrayal.
It was out of love that I sailed with my heart.
It is where she taught me to untie the knots of trauma,
to find my stars within when things get dark,
to be responsible for my own sails and
to trust my inner compass to guide me in the outer world.
These are lessons that have taught me
how to love truer, and deeper.
And I realized in following my soul's compass,
I discovered how to unconditionally love.

The sunrise calls

It takes courage the leave my self-imprisoned cages
to fly into the beauty of the sunrise.
And yet, the sunrise calls.
She hears my longing to be free
and shines the way each day.
She has led me out of...
-the cage of betrayal as I trusted my own wings.
-the cage of comparing myself with others as I chose to focus my own
gifts and learn their beauty.
-the cage of poverty as I came
to understand that every breath is a gift.
My breath is my constant companion
rising and falling with me on every step of my journey.
My sacred friend of constant support and connection to all.
I sit and watch the sunrise enlighten the wings of a bird as she
navigates between the sky and water.
I smile and breathe in the freedom found
from allowing the sun to rise within me.
Her light navigates me between my ego and my soul.
And as I breathe out,
I begin to wonder what cage I will free myself from today...

A doorway in...

It's a doorway in...
A doorway into joy.
The bougainvillea and breeze join together
dancing in delight that you have arrived.
The palms wave and invite you to lay by them and
let them cool you.
A bike awaits you to reclaim your innocence and
remember some of your first tastes of freedom.
Come on in...
We've missed you.

Soul speak

I'd like to:
Drop out of the Mind
Listen to the Heart
Connect with my Soul

So I:
Dance with the breeze
Float in the sea
Soak in the shine
Speak with the stars

Moon Smiles

Next to the palm, a tiny crescent moon smiles.
I wonder if she is smiling because she is a reminder
that no matter how dark it gets,
there is still light.
I wonder if she is smiling because
even though she seems to be just a small light
in the purple skies,
she still has the power to affect the tides of the sea.
She reminds me that even a small amount of light
holds the power to effect great change.
I wonder if she is smiling at me
because even though my mind thinks she is very far away,
I still feel her in me.
I feel Spirit smile.
I smile.
with the moon
with Spirt
All as One.

No pier pressure

Sometimes I've had to walk away from people
when my soul has had a growth spurt.
It's usually a grieving experience
mixed with anger, sadness, and fear on both sides.
For most of my life, I did not have the understanding
let alone the words to explain
that somehow I've grown out of the role I was playing with them.
As more of my soul took over,
my roles had to shed
and it now hurt to try and fit
into what used to be such a comfy space.
Kinda like trying to fit into my fourth-grade jeans.
No matter how much I loved those jeans
and how much I learned in them,
I've outgrown them and I have to let go.
I've noticed when I try to shrink myself to stay in relationships,
I'd hurt deep within
and often cause more distance with the person than needed to be.
Or maybe it had hurt that much as I loved them that much.
It is still mostly a mystery to me.
On days when my heart hurts for the past,
I like to find a quiet pier
and let go of the pressure of how I think things should be.
When I do, I can sense the understanding smile of our souls.
Down deep, we are not upset
but are all cheering one another on.
Grow dear friend... Grow.

Life Rings

Today I discover ways to take exquisite care of myself.
As I do, my heart sings
the song of my soul
and will gift others with her music.
My soul's music
will lift other hearts
like a life ring in turbulent waters
as your soul's music
has done for me.
Lifting. Encircling. Holding.

Colors of the Sea

If I could see the colors of my heart,
she would be colored like the sea

Sea the Power

Today I sit in gratitude for the sea and her power.
On most days, the sea wields her power by
giving a wave
and gently tickling my toes.
Her kindness offers me
a buoyancy from my heavy worries.
She inspires me to swim
deep into the ocean that lies within me.
In this depth, it is still.
I am home.
I thank her for her wisdom
reminding me that we are all seeking
a kind wave,
a way to rise from our heavy worries
and a little tickle of compassion.
Today, I offer just that to you.
A kind wave-
A prayer that your worries float away-
A reminder that you have
a still, loving place within you-

Sailing Soul

In this sunset, I felt my soul speak.
She spoke in waves that overtook my small vessel
and throw me into a bottomless unknown sea.
She cut me open and threw me in with bloodthirsty predators. She let me
fight, wail and rage until I had nothing left in me except to surrender.
It was in my surrender
that I felt as if I had read a million new books,
heard a choir of angels
and was able to see with new eyes.
I understood that it is all a gift.
I had to be lost, alone and attacked to let go
of who I thought I was supposed to be
and wake up to who I am.
I suddenly had a profound appreciation
that any and all methods necessary will be employed in love
to save me from myself.
I sat peacefully
looking back at the storm and let it be behind me.
The fears faded away with the misty clouds
leaving behind volumes of wisdom
and for the first time
loving back the love
that has always been there.

Overflowing Blessings

May your blessings
spill over all your walls you've built.

Necessary Ingredients

The butterfly said, "Dear flower -
I am here to honor your transformation.
I know your journey led you deep into darkness as a seed and
your outer shell was completely destroyed.
With your faith, I've watched you grow towards the light and rise
above the dirt into a whole new world.
I connect with you in the wisdom
that darkness and destruction
are necessary ingredients for growth.
I've delighted in your joyful dances with the breeze and peaceful
receiving of the gifts of the sun
since you burst into this world.
On this sacred day
of your first bloom,
we butterflies and bees celebrate
the ingredients you mix into life.
We regale in deep appreciation your gift of pollen that contributes
to the greater whole.
We sit in gratitude at the joy you provide to countless others with
just a glance at you.
Time to bloom dear one.

Combustive Passions

Today I listen to my passions deep within
and set them free.
My permission sparks a combustion
sending forth an inferno
that devours
my outgrown roles,
the voice of my wicked criticizer,
and my unhealthy expectations.
Scorching through who I built myself to be
to reveal who I really am.
Walking out the fire,
I am lighter.
It is time to rise.

Sand Goddess

Today I came upon the goddess of sand

formed by the sea

to greet the breeze.

She praised the wind for her global service.

The breeze then praised the sun

and the sun appreciated the sea.

I sat in awe as they each honored their ancient friendships.

Like old friends connecting again,

they laughed at the chaos they have been through

and regaled in tales of their creations together.

I became overwhelmed in gratitude for their

sacred interweaving connections and

collaborative universal service.

They are daily evidence of unconditional love for all.

Unitive Song

In this moment:

I notice the movement of the wind chimes

as they create songs with the wind.

I choose to connect with

and receive the gifts

of my chosen focus.

I hum to the wind chimes and become part of the music.

The wind,

the chimes

and me

sharing our separate gifts

to become a unitive song.

Waves of Compassion

I discovered there is a color in the sea
that sends compassionate waves through me.
It is though that color has a key that
unlocks parts of my heart
fiercely protected after
she has been stung.
Without a word,
she gently washes away the sting
with compassion
and I am at peace again.

Bella Pauses

Today's gratitude walk focused on Bella's pauses...
those moments that Bella stops our walks.
She refuses to leave,
takes her time,
and pauses to embrace life.
I found myself trying to hurry her along
and I then wondered…why I'm still rushing
in a stilled world?
Where is it I need to be?
The world has paused my patterns.
There is nowhere I HAVE to be right now.
As I sit in the discomfort that arises for me with this thought,
I realize my hurried pace gives my negative thoughts
the space they need to survive
because when I still…
peaceful thoughts take their place.
I realize I've been rushing past where I am
to where I think I need to be.
I smile at the inspired thought
that there is nowhere to be but
here.

Friends of Sunrise

As I watched the sunrise,
my heart opened by thinking,
the sun is rising for me.
As I revel in the colors it shines,
I recognize it is through my chosen focus,
the sunrise and I
are celebrating
a new beginning together.
The sea peacefully rose up to agree.
I then celebrated that the same sunrise
was inspiring another I have never met.
I smiled.
Blessings to you my friends of the sunrise.
Blessings to you my friends of new beginnings.
Blessings to you my friends of the sea.
May today you know that even if we never meet,
I am grateful to celebrate this sunrise
and a new beginning with you.

Deeper Peace

The sea and my soul both
hold more peace
the deeper I go.

Slowing Down

Our snail is back to remind me
to slow down.
I took in some deep breaths
as my dog Bella Grace said hello to the snail
and then took the time to smell the flowers around her.
As we walked down the blossoming streets,
I smiled at the smell of plumeria,
spun my gratitude ring
and felt my heart fill with gratitude.
Bella took off and chased an iguana up a tree
and as I got her to calm,
she sat bathed in light.
I took a moment
in meditation
to allow myself
to fill with light
and came home
feeling renewed
and overflowing with gratitude.

Helpful Tides

Today, I send my worries into the waves of the sea
and let the tides
find them a new place to dock.

green parrot bar

NO SNIVELLING SINCE 1890

601 Whitehead Street   KEY WEST

No Sniveling

I return from today's gratitude walk

in deep appreciation for Key West.

I've found the island to be a spiritual vortex

for healing my heart.

When I listen, the island reveals ways for me

to breathe,

to laugh,

to dance,

to flourish,

to celebrate,

to love and to shine.

I pass a reminder for "No Sniveling"

and choose to focus my thoughts on joy.

After all, it is hard to be a joyous sniveler.

Shine and Flourish

On today's grateful walk,
hope fills my heart
as I see an aura of light
around Our Lady of Lourdes.
She reminds me that at all times
there is at least someone praying around the world
for the good of us all.
We don't always know
where someone is praying
or who it is...
but that is the love of humanity in action.
I stop and pray:
May all be healthy
May all be safe
May all be free of suffering
May all flourish
May all find their love within and shine who they are

Shine and flourish today my friend.

Heart Smiles

I celebrate the colors of the bougainvillea
as they often make my heart smile
at their beauty.
I take extra time with them since I've discovered
how they make my heart smile.
A wise way to make my worries cease.

Simple Joys

I am grateful for Bella's smile each day.
She reminds me of joy
in such simple things
like the tickle of grass on her belly,
the peace brought by keeping your paws by the sea
and the importance of being bathed
in sunshine.

Exposed and Vulnerable Beauty

On my grateful walk during the pandemic,

I see three leaves that look like hearts.

They remind me that we are all connected

and growing together.

Just as nature finds a way, so will we.

Now, with more exposed hearts.

I humbly realize that it is in our vulnerable state

that we becoming

more connected,

stronger

and wise.

Sending you gratitude

for your exposed, vulnerable heart…

it is what changes the world for the better.

New Shores

May the storms we are weathering
guide us
into new shores
more beautiful
then we imagined.

Breathing Trees

Today I take time to breathe with a tree.
As Bella I sat with this royal poinciana,
I realized the tree breathes in
what I breathe out
and I breathe in
what the tree breathes out.
May today you breathe in the gifts of nature
and breathe out with love.

Charm and Magic

Today I find gratitude for the charm
and indescribable magic
that I've discovered in Key West.
As I sit with trying to put this love into words,
I landed on a mixture of how the sea air
has the power to blow away my anger,
the way the art speaks to my heart
in the way no words can describe
and the people
who still choose to spread joy and kindness.
I realize that as I focus on these gifts,
they soften the hard edges of trauma,
give me compassion for those I struggle with
and allow my clenched heart to let go and smile again.
Thank you for everyone who creates every kind of art
Thank you kind people
Thank you joyous people
Thank you eyes for the colors I see
Thank you sea air
Thank you Key West
Thank you Bella for bringing me on these gratitude walks

Discover More

www.gratefulwalks.com

All photos available on canvas
Please reach out to
connect@gratefulwalks.com
for more information.

Made in the USA
Las Vegas, NV
21 September 2023

77903130R00069